Praise for Sacrilegion

"Beware! Lamar Wilson's *Sacrilegion* is a land of terror: 'The man in the shack on the corner wants / to kiss you.' Relax. *Sacrilegion* is the most intimate of conversations: 'I am the what-are-you.' Ready your mind: 'Learn a strange language & its stranger / god.' Pray without ceasing: 'I am often left alone with my thoughts in my one good hand, / with this charge to keep, this god to glorify.' Over and again, these poems ask us to be ourselves and to rightly remember whatever land we thought of as home. Then they ask us to know homelessness, alienation, (dis)ability. This is a stunning debut doing what poetry must do; or as Lamar Wilson would say, 'Art does that to people. You get close enough to the texture / of the aquamarine & see the way it smacks the waves' crests, & man, / you can't help but melt into a puddle of when.'" —JERICHO BROWN

"*Sacrilegion* chants new songlines of the sacred and profane, radiating legions of regions we must all negotiate together. Love, life, identity and language wrestle and riff here with pure expressive power." —LEE ANN BROWN

"You who are looking…holding…questioning…embracing this book should take it home with you. Let it sing you to sleep. Let it call you awake. This is your book. Claim it." —NIKKI GIOVANNI

"In poems of great energy and sweep, I can feel Lamar Wilson coming in to his own, pushing against the limiting notions of others and developing faith in the truth and value of his existence. 'I am not afraid of facing you, or me, / or the notion of we the people anymore. I am your darker brother. / I am vast. I contain multitudes. / I am the what-are-you. / I am the brown, the red, the white, the sometimes blue. / & I am all-American. / What are you?' These are poems of embrace and indictment that churn with the force of revelation, and their beauty, their social relevance and challenge, comes from how personal, how honest he is willing to be." —BOB HICOK

"L. Lamar Wilson reinvents the memoir in verse with the tour de force of his *Sacrilegion*. With a keen eye that toggles between reverie and our hopes for the future, Wilson offers a salve for any soul that knows what it feels like to be counted out only to fight back toward resurrection. Few collections will move the spirit like this one; from its incantatory moments to those that speak in tongues, you believe, with every line, that this poet does 'feel everything every-where else / more than most.'" —A . V A N J O R D A N

"Open the pages of Lamar Wilson's stunning debut, *Sacrilegion*, and you will find 'a different kind of holy…a sacrament for our sanctifunked / souls,' where personal experience blends with the scars of collective historical injustice. Wilson's bold poetic voice calls out hymns of acceptance in the face of racism, homophobia, (dis)ability, and illness, and his big-hearted blessings cast their light over the wider world. These poems sing with authority, and sway with hard music of the body—the broken body, the erotic body, the scarred body, the holy body—and offer up redemption through God, love, and desire. 'O will we ever know how beautiful we are?' Wilson asks, and by the end of *Sacrilegion*, the answer is a resounding yes." —E R I K A M E I T N E R

"Lamar Wilson's *Sacrilegion* reminds us of what we already knew: that the body is a temple and that the spirit and the flesh—in this world, at least—are insepa-rable. Without judgment or shame, these poems walk us through the world we so blindly inhabit, illuminating the horrors and beauties hidden in the shadows, calling out the mysteries of desire in multiple tongues, singing praises to the divine that is here on earth as it is in heaven. Wilson's poems are as deeply felt as they are richly textured; his careful craft carries a heady, metaphysical freight. Look for his language to lick you: to bring you pleasure and to break you open. These are living words." —E V I E S H O C K L E Y

"In a world of intent on camouflage, where hearts thump beneath thin veneer and secrets are held tight to the chest, *Sacrilegion* roars through and burns the landscape flat, insistent on a new beginning. These unrelenting stanzas fling open closets, rip away masks and serve up unwavering queries for a deity who accepts and oversees the chaos. This volume is a gorgeously crafted fusion of reverence, intimacy and anger, stamped with the formidable signature of a poet whose talent is beyond question." —P A T R I C I A S M I T H

SACRILEGION

L. Lamar Wilson

Poetry Series #16

CAROLINA WREN PRESS
Durham, North Carolina

Series Editor: Andrea Selch

Design: Lesley Landis Designs
Cover Image and Author Photograph: Rachel Eliza Griffiths ©2013

The mission of Carolina Wren Press is to seek out, nurture and promote literary work by new and underrepresented writers, including women and writers of color.

Carolina Wren Press is a 501(c)3 nonprofit organization supported in part by grants and generous individual donors. In addition, we gratefully acknowledge the ongoing support of Carolina Wren Press's activities made possible through gifts to the Durham Arts Council's United Arts Fund and a special grant from the North Carolina Arts Council.

Library of Congress Cataloguing-in-Publication Data

Wilson, L. Lamar, 1979-
   [Poems. Selections]
Sacrilegion/ by L. Lamar Wilson
    pages. cm. -- (Poetry series ; #16)
ISBN 978-0-932112-93-4 (alk. paper)
I. Title

PS3623.I585464S23 2013
811'.6--dc23

2012047759

If this is arrogant, God, forgive me,
but this is what I need to say.
May what I do flow from me like a river,
no forcing and no holding back,
the way it is with children.

—RAINER MARIA RILKE

TABLE OF CONTENTS

Prelude: I Can't Help It

I talk too much. I cannot tell a liar
from a preacher, so I tell you
what you want: I'm saved & sick
of this world, safe in God's arms. God,
give me this world in an honest man's
arms. An ego is hard to stroke. Or easy if
you know how to quiet it, let a man feel
his burn in your throat. I talk too much.
I'm sorry I'm not sorry enough. I'll dance
all over you. O liar. Preacher. Daddy-
o, your tongue lashing is never hard
or fast enough. When you lie still,
stroking your chalice, the quiet makes me
retch. I am a lone dandelion in a field,
waiting. Come. Blow me to bits. Still.
You'll die this way, saved by the lies
that burn like the ice water & alcohol
Mama sits me in to break the fevers
our silences brought. I'll die thrashing,
telling any body all my secrets.

I

I got the love of Jesus
I got the love of Jesus
I got the love of Jesus
in my heart

Times Like These: Marianna, Florida

One woe is past; &, behold, there come two woes more hereafter.
—Revelation 9:12

In one field, husks, muscadine vines & a sugarcane graveyard furrow acres aching for the devil to beat his wife. In another, a skein of maggots & mayflies, musk thick & resolute, jockey for the cow's afterbirth. Down Old U.S. Road, weevils wheeze & chafed bales of hay settle for the wind's sneezes. *Wait for a sign,* the couple says & set their table with damask, fresh-pressed for a feast of sardines & cornbread. Train their child in the way he should babble. From dusk till dusk, they lull the boy with tales of a faraway sea, buckets of oysters to shuck. *OurFatherwhichartinheavenhallowedbe thynamethykingdomcomethywillbedoneonearthasitisinheaven.* Still no rain. From dusk till dusk, they till dust. They reach for the locks of hair & black-eyed peas, stowed away for times like these.

Woe Unto You, Sons

You can't cry blood, Daddy says
on the ride home from school.
You sulk, face in hand, recall
the locker room circle. *Yes, I love*
hopscotch. No, I don't want to,
you know, her. His laughter slaps
your cheek like an open hand
as he pats your shoulder. *Learn*
to lie, son. Lick the salty stream
as it drips from nose to philtrum to lip.

What of a Body

that cannot lie,
of sinews that do not obey
when commanded to cease
their quaking? What
of a body that scoffs
at holy water's
conditions, of pores
that hunger for
a tongue's fetter,
of nerves deaf
to homilies of *sweet
by & by & batty bwoy,
boom bye bye*? Who
can hold this body
in his hands, silence
its tender, muted moan
beneath scars
that will not heal?

Family Reunion, 1993

When I am asked whose tears these are, I always blame the moon.
—Lucille Clifton

I give my cousin my hand & think
of the year before, how he'd held me aloft,

his bicep pulsing against the weight
of my bones & adoration. *Can I get it*

by touching him? I wonder but don't speak,
don't let go until his slick flesh kisses

the commode, then trace curlicues & stars
into my stucco canvas amid his grunts & sighs,

stare at the moon I've made there as full of itself
as the one that had shone on us at the reunion,

our mothers in orbit around us in their own groove
with Frankie Beverly. *I'm flying!* I had beamed

at myself, gilded in his tooth: the only
shimmering thing in this dark, damp silence.

It Could Happen to Anyone:
A Letter to the Boy

The man in the shack on the corner wants
to kiss you. He remembers when you jump-roped
better than most of the girls & prayed without
manly pretense, remembers how you mimicked
the church mothers—*knees & body bowed, Lawd*—
your genuine contrition for being broken
& breakable still. *You always was too pretty
to be a boy. Come gimme some sugar,* he says,
& reaches out to kiss you on your cheek, but
his lips are thistles, his face a cavern of bones.
It's World AIDS Day, & you are here to report
his free fall from engineer to blind man leading
the myope, to fevers that flash on & off like a switch
spooked by the God he calls *great & merciful*
with a smile. Your mother says his songs tore up
church services all over town like hurricanes
had done Old U.S. Road: limbs splayed,
stripped bare, convulsing like saints slain
by spirits he conjured. You don't remember,
so busy kneeling at the altar of this you the mothers
& sanctified brothers could praise, who loved
Shirts Against Skins more than Bible study,
loved tackling the most buff Skin on the field,
who always held you on top of him long
enough for you to feel him hardening against you
hardening. *Gimme some skin, nigga,* he'd say,
& grin, as you pulled away, then reached to pull
him to his feet. This man doesn't know the you
who dreamed of kissing the lead tuba player
but was too much of a punk or a saint or both

to follow his leer from dais to bathroom stall.
It could happen to anyone, he says, *especially
when you love somebody. Make sure
you write that down.* You don't. Too
sentimental, you think, for a hard
news story, so you dig for the grit, for the who
who branded him untouchable. He smiles,
places one hand on his chest, gropes the table
for yours. *You using protection with these boys?*
His scaly palm grazes your keloid knuckles.
I haven't, you know, yet, you mumble, happy
for once to be numb, glad you can't feel the heat.

What Did You Do to Yourself?: Finding Fault

I was born & lived to darn
myself a cocoon. I don't feel a thing
in my left hand in here, but I used
to feel everything everywhere else
more than most. God said
let there be irony & there was I:
fighting the doctor's forceps
on my coming out day. The preacher says
In all things give thanks, & I do.

Thank you, God, for this holy bum hand.

It's nice to be able to hurt myself
& not have to take the blame.
Yesterday, I burned my ring finger
into a bloody mess. It's been burning
for a studded companion for years.
Or at least I think it has. I can't
be sure, but where I'm from,
I couldn't marry who I want anyway.
The preacher says this desire
is unnatural. *Gawd don't make*
no mistakes! Gawd don't like ugly!

Thank you, God, I am an unnatural beauty.

I've felt this desire as long as I've not felt
my pinky, long before I broke it
doing exercises the good doctor
told me would help me feel again,
the one that's still broken

because no one noticed & I've learned
it's easier to let you forget, to sing.
I wish some pervert had touched me
when I was 6 or 17. Then I'd have
someone else to share this blame.
Every Sunday, we sing *Yes, Jesus loves me*
to the children & I cry. I stopped asking
the preacher if his god loves me & my hand
years ago. I intuited early I couldn't trust
his truths. Little J's eyes light up
every time I walk into the sanctuary.

Thank you, God, I am not a pervert.

Resurrection Sunday

A man holds his penis in his mouth.
Sprawled on a cheap sofa like the one
that holds my bare backside, he stares blankly

through the lens at the director for his cues,
through me reaching for his gaze. I'm twentysomething
& home alone. I'm so there. I'm so not there

or here alone. See the boy in overalls: cross-legged
& wedged in the corner between two walls
of books. He stares as Claude Neal's limp tongue

holds his own limpness on the fading page
of one dusty tome, Claude's sockets fixed
on some constellation the boy wishes

he could decipher. Claude's body—chiseled
& mangled—hangs in an oak by a rope. There is nothing
in this body we can desire, & we want.

We want a body, not mangled like ours,
we can love without shame. The boy feels
so small in his body, its scars that beckon

stares & gasps. I am he, doubled in size
& solemnity. I churn. I am an ocean
of want. This video's hustler must do.

His left pec brandishes a lion's paw
& skull-&-bones. A broken heart heaves outside
his right. With each kiss, our heads swell.

He'll make $250 for this trick, $150 more
than he'd earn trading others in parked cars
on a street corner where no trees will grow,

all these miles from us. This director promises
he's stardust, has the blow to get him to the edge
& may actually finish him. He tells him,

tells me, what to do next, moans *Big.*
Black. Cock. I obey. I swell more still
& remember I should be studying

what Nietzsche says God isn't. I am
at a black university. God always
enters the classroom here,

& my professor, a newly converted
agnostic, will prove her theories. But
this video's lessons will pay off sooner

& take me & this boy closer than when
he stared at Claude, hanging, in *The Anatomy*
of a Lynching on that long ride home from the library,

squinting but unable to see Claude's pupils, see
if peace eclipsed terror before he died. *Child,*
they came from everywhere & all you could do was pray

you weren't the nigger they picked for the picnic
on the courthouse lawn, our grandmother says.
In the picture, Claude is alone, but as she speaks,

kids blur into the sepia background, ape
the grins on their parents' faces, await
their turn to prod his charred flesh.

The boy asks if Claude was a good student
like him, if she was the one who would not give
the NAACP her name when 50-cent postcards,

news of Claude's fingers & toes for sale
reached stands. *I told that boy to leave*
that white gal alone: the only words

breaking the silence of the rest of that ride,
the only words her brother says at home.
I told that boy to leave that white gal alone:

their script a shroud over faces suddenly
childlike, each crease around their eyes
a dog-eared page the boy can never read.

The boy wants to ask where the family
of Lola, Claude's slain lover, lives, where
his pickled prick must collect dust

on some shelf. He wants to say *I want*
to study it. He wants to see how he'd hang,
loosed to rove in a bottle. But he is a boy.

He does not know how to speak
the unspeakable yet. I
heave. It is almost dawn now.

The courthouse towers there,
in the center of that town, & that oak,
mostly limbless, looms.   Still.

Soon, its flaccid branches will shade
more brown boys, guilty or not, waiting
to learn what their next move will be. It's hard

to get anywhere without passing it, passing them,
bowed, not meeting our gaze. The hustler moans.
I gasp. I cannot take this boy, this fallen porn star

or his unseen master's plan where I'm bound.
I turn off the TV. I am not afraid to raise
this dead flesh, for all & no one to see, alone,

like that other hanged man the boy followed
so slavishly, to ask him what no man,
not even Daddy, can show me: Jesus,

if a man is black & his manhood is forced
into his own mouth by another man
who's as afraid of the power he holds

but is pale enough to hold the camera
or the noose, how much of a man isn't he?
Like you, O Lord, I rise with all power

in my hand, but I do not want to cross
this tempest alone. I am not that boy
anymore. I am not afraid to say

I am a man, searching for a man
whose flesh will rise, only for me,
without force, without fear. Come,

lie with me & be redeemed. See
my yoke, this flesh, broken
for you? Find here

a different kind of holy, a sacrilegion,
a sacrament for our sanctifunked
souls. Dark & darker.   Still.

II

Millions
didn't make it
but I was
one of the ones
who did

Lost & Found in Tallahassee

Eres uno de nosotros! the old women chant as they circle
me at the center table. Their molasses hands smooth

my pimply cheeks. *You are one of us!* they sing, the beat
of their pattering feet in sync with my quaking knees.

They have journeyed from Nacimiento to thank students
who have decided to civilize them. *Eres un Mascogo,*

says one who looks like my grandmother's sister. *You are
a black Seminole.* She traces the scars on the hand

that will not move, that I try to hide, speaks of a home
I never knew I knew. What to say? *Soy un americano*

negro, I mumble. *Esto es nuestro hogar, también,* she hums.
This is not your home, too. This is not the story I have memorized.

I am a reporter, here to capture a tale of new sewer lines
& streetlights that will make her blue-black face shine.

¿Qué se les gustaria decir a los estudiantes? I probe again.
I need a soundbite, groveling that fits the news I must print.

I do not tell her she is mocked across this city's tracks with
a *Hey-ya-hooo!* & fake war paint. I do not have to. My pen is running

out of ink. My rehearsed accent fails. Her eyes wrinkle into smiles.
Eres uno de nosotros! Eres uno de nosotros! Eres uno…

We Do Not Know Her Name

I do not know her name, but without her,
I do not have a name. No name, no face,

no place with your people, my people. You
have forgotten me, the tawny one, like my great-

grandmother, like Chief Osceola's wife Morning Dew,
forgotten the drops of my blood—her blood mixed with his,

with yours—how you fought for her honor,
because we were wronged, together. My hero,

your Osceola, loved his Morning Dew,
got her brothers—my ancestors

& yours—to soak the Florida soil, the Georgia clay,
with a richer red. Her seeds, your seeds, legion.

Don't remember that now? How we wandered
with you along rivers History reduced to a trail,

made new homes in Okeechobee swamps, Oklahoma
& Mexico deserts. Learned Cherokee, French & Spanish.

History's dead now. My grandfather's mother—
she's dead, too. No name, no face, no place

with my people. You. Only a figment
of her daughter-in-law's fading memory,

glaucoma & dementia clouding visions
of hair that crowned breasts & hips like a halo.

You have forgotten me. You have voted
me away from the land our blood bought.

You don't remember that now,
either. We do not know our names.

Drapetomania: Morning Dew

If I kill these white men, can I go home to my husband?
If I kill these white men, can I go home to my people?
If I kill these white men, I can go home to my people.
If I kill these white men, I can go home to my husband.
When I kill these white men, I will go home to my husband.
When I kill these white men, I will go home to my people.
When I kill these white men, I will never leave my people.
When I kill these white men, I will never leave my husband.
I have killed these white men; they will come for my husband.
I have killed these white men; they will come for my people.
I have killed these white men; they will kill my husband.
I have killed these white men; they will kill my people.
If I kill myself, will I end this war? If I kill myself,
I will end this war. I must kill myself. I must kill myself.

You Da Only Man I Loves, Daddy:
Lot's Daughters

The things that you're liable to read in the Bible,
it ain't necessarily so.
—Ira Gershwin

How you gon' let dem strangers touch me, Daddy?
How you gon' let dem strangers touch me?
You say only you can touch me, Daddy, 'member?
You say only you can touch me.

You say we can' let my coat tear up too soon, say
We can' let it tear up, you say
We can' let my coat tear up too soon, say
We can' let it tear up, say

If it do no man will want me, you say
If it do no man will want me, say
If it do no man will want me, you say
If it do no man will want me

Guess it don' matter now, do it?
Guess it don' matter now? Funny how
It jus' don' matter now? Funny how
It jus' don' matter now

Mama done gon' off & left us, Daddy
Look like Mama done gon' off & left us, wonder why
Mama done gon' off & left us, Daddy, wonder why
Mama done gon' off & left us

You da only man I loves, Daddy, you know
You da only man I loves, sho' nuff
You da only man I loves, Daddy, you know
You da only man I loves

Now I gon' have yo' babies, Daddy
Now I gon' have yo' babies, so glad
Now I gon' have yo' babies, Daddy, so glad,
Now I gon' have yo' babies

Picky: Izola Ware Curry

In the end
Tarzan always get hold of Jane
& what I'm tryin' to figure
is how he swing
on them vines & know
which of them gals
can hold him fast
& not take him out
on the wrong limb
how he land so soft like
not a speck of sweat on his flesh
like them peaches where I come from
you got to be careful which one
you bite into even if it
look like it sweet as cane
could be a worm or worse inside
grinnin' at you like you
the unexpected guest so
when I went to the picture show
to get out the house & stopped by
the store to hunt for some work
or a smile or two & I saw this
boy & his mob callin' him a king
Arthur Lucer I think
which sound like Lucifer to me
& when I got up close enough
to look him in his eyes,
he looked at me like I was common
as all the rest he got hold of, like
he sho' did seem to know too much
about where I been & talk
about a freedom he knew
I ain't never gonna see so
right then I knew it was him
or me gonna take a stab
at livin' another day &
just this one time
I chose me

An Atlanta Hustler Confesses to Lawyers
Before Requesting the Death Penalty

They all asked me to use a tie on 'em. I swear. Said they liked not being in control.
I could always tell their kind. Gaunt & thick in the lips like they'd just learned
to pout. Out of place in the fog of Timbs, hoodies & cock rings in Bulldogs,
in their Mr. Rogers blazers & khakis, coming to teach us to be good neighbors.
Always walking with their asses jutted out like they're balancing a vase
of daffodils. Begging to buck at my will. To breathe as I order. To stop.
I swear his tie looked like it had a Matisse I saw at the High once on it.
I get art just like any other Joe I blow off. I ain't no dummy, you know?
I met him early that afternoon. He lived a couple miles from the bar
in the Belvedere. Said he'd had a long day at the office. Decided to reward
himself with some sexual healing. I've always loved that song. Nothing
like Marvin to get you in the mood to snort some Tina & blast off to Mercury
& back. Didn't take long for him to come after I wrapped Matisse around
his wrists. Art does that to people. You get close enough to the texture
of the aquamarine & see the way it smacks the waves' crests, & man,
you can't help but melt into a puddle of when. When you want
to scream, but you're nothing but gasps & goosebumps. I pulled the knot
real tight, rammed in, & in 30 seconds, I swear, he was done. The first time.
But he wanted it again. *Wake up! Wake up! Wake up!* Easiest trick I ever made.
He said he had it, too. Said we could fuck raw. That's why this trial don't
mean shit. Just let me shoot up on some of that laughing gas & take off.
That's what he would have wanted for me. For the both of us. I could see
he was ready, so I balled the end of the pillowcase & stuffed it in his mouth.
His eyes rolled back as he moaned, begging for my hand around his throat.
I made a fist. Held him. Steadfast. He shook like a wild cock rung out
for supper. *Shut up, boy!* & he did. Like I did. I always was a good boy.

HeLa

for Henrietta Lacks

I won't die. I keep
white men up at night. I come
from the deepest basin
they know. They want
to watch me grow
so they took me from
Mama. When they hold
me close, it's always
so cold, but when Sister came
to see me the other day,
she kissed me & called me
beautiful & I was warm again,
like it always was with Mama,
just for a little while.
Yemoja olodo awoye Yemoja…

I—two, one hundred,
three million, legion, spawn
of gall, glory of silt
gone sour—make the slack-jawed
bow & wish they could drink
from my ever-after. Now these men
have brought women friends
to look at me. They say I'm getting
stronger every day. They want
me to tell them my secrets, but
I don't know what they mean.
How can I explain who
I am if they can't see,
after looking at me? They call
me HeLa. Healer. Mama
would be proud to know
we got healing in us. I hope
she understands I didn't want
to go… *Yemoja Orisha Orisha*
Yemoja fun me lowo. Asé. Asé.

Drive-by

Bah daaaaaah! Bah daaaaaah! Bah doo dah! Dah dah daaaah dee daaaaaah! Bah daaaaaah!

Must be the dread-
    locks, no, the red-hot SUV, no
the deer-in-headlights glare after
    a rear-end accident, the shock
of the hit-&-run, the latest irony of my existence
    since my brachial plexus snapped
& left me a palsied leper.

    Bah daaaaaah! Bah daaaaaah! Bah doo dah! Dah dah daaaah dee daaaaaah! Bah daaaaaah!

Must be that I am too
    helpful to Miss Gold-Star Gumshoe.
Must be hiding something be-
    hind my eagerness to hand over Florida
registration & grinning license pic,
    riding through this side of Milwaukee's worst
at 2 a.m. *I had a gig on*

32nd & Burleigh, I muster,
    pointing to a beat-up trumpet case, but
Jazz? Cannot be that simple.
    We just need to take you in to check things out.
I remain silent.
    Bah daaaaaah! Bah daaaaaah! Bah doo dah! Dah dah
    daaaah dee daaaaaah! Bah daaaaaah!
    wailing inside on the ride to the precinct, where

Turn! Flash *Turn!*
    Flash *Turn!* Flash
welcomes me. Steeled into submission, I
    sleep. Four hours pass. I awake, railing

Why am I still here? Why am I still
    here? Why... Reluctantly, I
am released.

        Bah daaaaaah! Bah daaaaaah! Bah doo dah! Dah dah daaaah dee daaaaaah! Bah daaaaaah!

Now, I seethe every drive-by, your
    public service announcement, the roar
of your sirens. The red, white & blue, flashing, threatens
    my sable soul, today, on this mountain. I want to die, no,
kill a little more each time you hover,
    searching for the next one of us to put away.

        Bah daaaaaah! Bah daaaaaah! Bah doo dah! Dah dah daaaah dee daaaaaah! Bah

I Am Black & Comely

I am black & comely, Solomon said, except
in King James' version. There, a *but* abuts
comely, making black less so, palatable. That beaut's
mind lured more women into his court than I suspect
that fair(y) James ever cared to see. Expecting
a real mama, whore or not, would feel the cut
of the sword long before its blade was sought,
Solomon saw division a perfect divining rod. Yet
his progeny—with as much sense as he,
& so much of it opaque in our holiest of holy
scripts—dare not question the sleight
of ~~James'~~ God's scribes' pens, the *buts* blighting
our wizened faces, making half-truths seem far
more palatable. O will we ever know how beautiful we are?

Legion: Human Immunodeficiency Virus

Return to thine own house, and shew how great things
God hath done unto thee.—Luke 8:39

Nothing's ever dead in a graveyard.
When you cry out for God, for touch,
our father who is not in heaven
or hell but in every body will send me.
When I'm with you, I'm only with you.
When I'm with her, I'm only with her
& you. When you're with him, I'm only with you & him & her & him
& him & her & him & you & her & him & her & him & you & her & him & you &
him & her & him & you & her & him & her & him & her & him & her & him &
her & him & your mama & him & her & daddy & her & you & him & him & her & you &
her barber & him & her & her & him & her & your neighbor & you & her & him & his professor
& her & her twin brother & him & your stylist & her & her & her favorite teacher & him & her
& him & her & him & her last date & him & him & her & him & you & her & him & his best friend &

When you are alone & cannot be stilled,   you & her husband's
I will never leave: my hands, your hands: him & her & him &
your blood's taint coursing: your high-   & her & his brother &
yellow heart's flesh hunger for bodies bruised her grandmother &
blue: who can h   her & him &

him & her & him &
boyfriend & him &
her girlfriend & him
him & him & her &
you & her & him &

her & her & your cousin &

him & your cousin &

her sister & her & his nail tech & him & her & him & you & her & her & him & her pastor & him & her & her uncle & her & him & you & her & her plumber & you & her godfather & him & her & him & you & her & his stepdad & her & her boss & her & her & him & you & her & him & her & him & you & her & your dentist & him & her & him & you & him & her & him & how could you? you didn't even know his name & him & her & him & her & him & you & you'll spend the rest of your life wondering why & him & her & him & her & her & him & her & him & we are still dying in shame & you are numb & her & him & you & her & him & her & him & a cold Saturday morning & you were bored & him & her & him & him & her & him & her & how could you? you didn't even know his name & him & her & her & him & her & in your mama's house you swept & washed Saturdays away & you & her & him & her & him & while ReRe wailed if you won't let me & her & him & her & him & her & you & her & we are dying shamed are you numb & her & him & you & her & him & her & him & her & enough to tell her this man didn't even come & her & him & her & him & you & her & him & with flowers or tales of a desire to kiss the groom & you & her & him & her & him & you & her & how could you? you didn't even know his name & him & her & her & him & her & you closed your eyes when he eased inside & wandered & him & you & her & him & her & him & wondered what D.J. stood for soaked through & him & you & her & him & her & him & you & we are still a shame to him & her & numbed to fear & her & him & you & her & him & her & him & you were open & you break easily when cold & her & him & her & her & him & you & her & him & come Saturday he'll find you walled in & you & her & him & her & him & you & there ain't no way for you to love you & him & her & him & her & him & her & him & you & how could you? you don't even know your name now & her & you & him & him & her & him & you & we are dying ah this shame we are numb & him & her & you & you &

III

*The blood
that gives me strength
from day to day*

Touch: A Letter to the Mother

I've driven 654 miles without sleep to make you better,
but when I ask how you feel & you thrust your breast
within my grasp & say *See, it's fine,* I see it's not. *Cool!*
I lie, then recoil. But you never have. Not when I came
to you, instead of Daddy, to show hair *down there.* Not
when I followed you, finally bra-free, to the bathroom
during commercial breaks to debate whodunit on *The Young
& the Restless* or to ask which jeans best showcased my assets.
Not when I danced around the house *naked as a jaybird,*
you'd say, never laughing at my *Funny Girl* monologues.
You didn't turn me away when I said *His name is Johnnie
& I love him,* & you never said *Brown boys can't be sissies, baby,*
though I wish you had, since now a lump the size of the head
of a tack may take away the only one who hasn't recoiled
at what comes naturally to me. Your eyes mirror mine
at the sight of what something so small can do: like a lump,
like a lie. *You're OK, it's OK* slips from my lips & I reach
out & touch your scar to assure us the enemy lurking
will not bring shame where shame has no home.

Chooseday!

My grandmother towers in the rocking chair like one of the live oaks
in her front yard, toned calves & freckled face defying time's

best efforts to dry-rot her. She lifts me from her lap as we finish
perfecting the vowel sounds in *teacher & orange*. I'll wow Mrs. Paramore

tomorrow with my elocution. *You speak so well,* she'll say, as she has
each day this term, & again, I won't feel her words' backhanded

sting. I've been bored with phonics for months, thanks to this retiree
too stubborn to fade quietly into a memory as other self-respecting

teachers have. *It's Chooseday!* we shout, mocking her friend, Miss Kiss,
recently felled by senility & snuff. I bolt up the concrete slabs & miss

MaMary's labored rise, her foot not quite swift enough to best
the top step, the wafting of collards & just-right cornbread clouding

her better judgment. It only takes a *Lawd, ham mercy!* for me to look back
& see her act her age. I sprawl, arms wide as I can stretch them,

awaiting the embrace of seven decades of balancing acts going kaput
on the linoleum. We laugh until breathless, squirm our way to our feet,

hand in hand. O for the days when my arms were enough to hold
her up, before her mind began erasing her mind & her sense of humor.

I watch her now, slumped in a wheelchair at the dinner table, her home away
from her hospital bed, hip & femur tender from falls on Tuesdays I wasn't there

to break them, mumbling an ancient tongue she's recalled, answering a voice
in the chasm she keeps her cataracts fixed on. She lifts her right hand.

Her offering: a sliver of the tablecloth, her third sacrifice this week. *Stop, baby!*
I chide, grabbing her hand, grinning. *It's only Chooseday!* Her face is as blank

as Mrs. Paramore's chalkboard on days I was monitor. *Who are you?*
she scowls. I stare back into the mirror that is her eyes & try not to slip.

Ghazal of the Naptime Blues

Every day after school, I savored my grandmother's fatback;
hints of Karo & margarine in the mix to pull the collards' bite back.

Tudda, MaMary's sister, finished supper with a can of beets:
May-ree, you sho' put yo' foot in dem greens, gurl, she'd pipe back.

Each idled to her chamber of secrets fading, stroked jet black wig,
freed sterling plaits, cleared talcum as freckles brought a schoolgirl spice back.

I tiptoed to spy this transformation, widow to ingénue, as one, then
the other, shut her eyes, rocked slowly, calling juke joint sights back.

MaMary took the bass line, Tudda alto's echo & I the tenor notes;
How *My mama done tol' me when I was in pigtails* comes right back

& I, your charge, long to lie at your feet, caress calico shag rugs,
hum naptime lullabies. Bring the *blues in the night* back!

Life After Death

for Tudda

Like the muscadine vines
you once sheared to canopy,
your bronze baby sags.

Not the breast who lost her twin
years ago to warring cells, but I—
who saw monolith, saw God & age defied

by your resolute spine, your silent
mourning—hang low. How you'd stuff
pads into bra, fill the missing mass

that had swelled when even young men
marveled at your eighty-something sashay,
the Piggly Wiggly your runway.

Eldorado Marie Long Grandberry Smith,
MaMary would scoff, *Please*
try to act yo' age, gurl!

Sheeeeeeeeeeeit! I'ma pop my coattails,
& all you hincty heifas can shrivel up
& die for all I care. Watch & weep!

I do now. I watched you, mute
in those last days, praying your wit,
stolen by summer, a stroke, would part

contorted lips & sing curses again.
Seeing you, frozen in this too-earnest box,
this failed resurrection, I remember still.

How proud calls from Chitown & Philly, L.A.
& Chocolate City made you, how you ate up
tales tall & wild & ripe as your favorite tree's fruit.

How you knew I wanted to be here, trimming
these vines, sucking juice from lustrous skin, shooing
bees & hummingbirds, waxy leaves dancing.

Now I hear you cackle *You mannish boy, I don't
care,* hear my eager tongue Charleston into night.
O why did I leave you & her here to wither?

I swell, burst & shimmy, waiting in this brush
for you to whack headless this serpent whose sleep
I've rattled, then kiss my forehead in the setting sun.

A Patch of Blue in Tenleytown

She ambles about this Mickey-Dee kitchen's din,
unmoved by the hot grease threatening
her *¿puedo tomar su orden?* mask.

No one is supposed to see it here.
A port-wine patch covers the left side of her face
from lash to lip. She's focused, unblinking.

Ah, I know this face, its smile a guise
I've mastered since I anchored the front row
of my pre-K graduation pic, gummy grin thrust

in front of awkward contortions
of a humerus bone my sky-blue gown
could not hold in place, shoulders propping

a hunched neck, arched vertebrae defying
scoliosis's grip, hoping no one would notice
the remnants of a failed surgery dimpling

my knuckles like train tracks dividing the haves
& never-wills in a town on a Deep South road
to nowhere. She catches me staring, & I wave

my limp wrist, an SOS. We burst into laughter,
instant *familia* in this part of this town eager to forget
it's below the Mason-Dixon line, &

designed by one brilliant black man's mind, one
who knew how to keep enemies out. She pushes
her hair back to show off her patch of blue,

waves both hands wildly. *Esa sonrisa ir, por favor!*
I want to say but instead order *dos bocadillos*—
all I can afford. Now we must say goodbye

& return to lives among those who aren't
in our tribe. I take one last glance at heaven's kiss
on her peach-pit flesh—mirror image of God,

of a schoolboy's stance—wave again, then
leave humming Celia's "No Encuentro Palabras"
for *mi hermana* all the way home.

In Search of Abe in Dupont Circle

Men, women & in-betweens hold
hands, walk too close, sport heels,

ass-out jeans, crew cuts & spurs
& cackle at will as you & I skip

into the bookstore. Our prize:
The Intimate World of Abraham Lincoln,

that treasure detailing the years before
his politics put Springfield on the map

& that silly top hat on his head, years
when he shared his bed with Joshua Speed—

whether because of tough times or a need
for companionship no one is certain.

But he did write him letters signed
Yours forever, & he did make room

in his presidential suite for David Derickson
when Mary Todd was away. She bore

Robert, Eddie, Willie & Tad & watched
two die before adolescence as Abe grew

more distant. *No wonder she went insane!*
you marvel as we meander past dildos & pornos

to the area marked HISTORY against the rear
wall near the register. We're sure we'll find him here.

But it's just another biography that doesn't tell
the rest of his story, our story. *Buy it anyway!*

you say, tracing each of my fingertips.
We set off marching with Abe to 17th & M

in our own little demonstration, laughing
at how phallic the Big Dipper looks tonight,

knowing we'll get to say I do
to whom we want one day. You

open the B&B door for me & laugh
as the lobby becomes catwalk. I look down,

& in my arms, Abe's eyes suddenly glint
against moonbeams & lamplight, seem sadder

than usual. I lose my balance & fall
against the elevator door, against you

waiting, holding it. You see what I can't say
& grab my listless hand, swoon about you

& your woman, about Jason & me, our
bicoastal, piecemeal family, woven together

without pomp, by circumstance. Our
delicate tapestry unfolds as you lift

my T-shirt over my head & we slip
into bed, warm skin warmer now: still:

surer of its holy. Then, I envelop you,
rub your bald head & surrender to your visions

of a day when a femme stud like you,
like Sakia Gunn, can strut down any street

with their women or punks like me
without the specter of a knife, of a hand

with no love for itself or the love it upends.
When I call that man who's said he loves me

for 102 days now—a feat as unprecedented
as believing he & I will wed & raise the child

I want you & me to make—& he doesn't answer,
you hum bars of Atlantic Starr's *Always,* shoo

the haints & omens in our commune, place my hand
on your belly, coo our waiting cherub to sleep.

Dreamboys

My nephew waltzes beside his father,
the man who was the boy who made *Faggot!*
a reason not to flinch. His neck a merry-

go-round, our boy rears back, waves
his pointer in my face, jabs his other fist
into his hip & wails: *Watch yo' mouth!*

Watch yo' mouth, Miss Effie White! 'Cause I
Don't take no mess from no second-rate diva
Who can't sustain! In my brother's eyes, I see

the pain of remembering when I crooned—*Don't*
tell me not to live. Just sit & putter. Life's candy
& the sun's a ball of butter—& made him grimace.

I scan the wall of plaques in Mama's den,
the remnants of home runs & aces that gave
him hope then, all dusty now. Teeth clenched,

he smiles at his dreamboy & nods in disbelief.
Harrumphs. Lashes flittering, he offers me
the only penance he can: a sheepish grin.

We applaud & feign heartened laughter.
My nephew sees beyond the veil shrouding
his father's eyes. Realizes this isn't

how brown boys win favor. Searches
my eyes for answers. Mirrors
a sadness no song can shake.

In the Lion's Den

hip pads & girdled pecs
strap-ons & cock rings
cough syrup & syringes
ecstacy & viagra

all night long
we sweat patrón out under strobes
glow, sniff, pop, prick,
swallow, don't spit out the seeds

bathe in rupaul's orders
ape beyoncé's buck
pimp tupac's swagger

you better work, bitch
faggot, punk, bulldagger, dyke
come get some of this thug passion, baby
uh-oh, uh-oh, uh-oh, oh, no, no

when sunday silences
the lion's den, we stumble
into holy pews & *Amen!*
news of our brimstone destiny

from the man we just saw
on all fours in the basement
moaning *more, sir, more...*

we weep as he reads
king james' script
then leave & follow another

handed down through generations
upon generations of *shalom & penzi*
pooling, warming our veins

lord, how oft shall
my brother sin against me
& i forgive him?

endow us with a deeper love
like stephen—his last breath
amid the torrent of stones

What I Should Have Told the Homeless Man in Cleveland Who Mistook Me for Mary's Son

Jesus, Jesus, Jesus ... By the time I hear it,
I have passed the beggar by three long strides,
sashaying in low-rise jeans like Tudda taught
me, accenting the hips Mama brought me. Soon,
I will bask in an estrogen sea at the House of Blues.
I think he's talking to you. Instantly, I am wailing
during midweek prayer meeting, the mothers' cries
lifting my petitions. *O Lord, I want to be like you. O
Lord, I want to know your heart. O Lord, I want
your thoughts to be mine. None but the righteous
shall see God,* they moaned on those hot summer nights,
their savior some no-count man who ran off & left
them, making me want him all the more. Who knew
I'd find him here, prostrate, before me? How sweet
this sound, this fallen soldier's plea for penance
on this corner of Euclid Avenue: his insanity my salvation.
I am born again. Our heads crane, mouths agape, both begging
for communion. I want to cradle his palms, whisper words
only he & I hear. Instead, I mouth *Bless you,* a half-smile
my only sacrament, then lock arms with my stunned friends
as we make our way to hear Floetry's love letters. But
what I should have told the homeless man in Cleveland
who mistook me for Mary's son is: I am not the man you seek.
I turn water into ice. I will never forsake my mother,
will never follow our father's edicts. I will kiss a man
tonight, but some would not call it holy. He will flay
my flesh with the tip of his tongue, & we will dance
until I ache as I worship earnestly on my knees.

Ratiocination

Outside looking in, I cannot place you,
though your breath tickles the hairs
in my nose each night. They will not go away

no matter how often or how closely I clip them,
& you will not let me penetrate you no matter
how many times you let me penetrate you.

You smile in your sleep more than you smile
when you are awake, & I like to watch you
from this distance. This must be how mercury feels

deep inside the heart of this red & brown clay
beneath us: deadly when we taste its ruddy gray, slick-
hot as that planet closest to the sun, hidden

from Earthly view by that star that burns
all flesh it touches & eludes us all.

You are soil, like me. Roiled
& sullen, like me. Together,
we cannot bear fruit. O lover,

in this full moon light, teach me how
to hide inside the embrace
of three-quarter you,

half-you, quarter-

you, full of me.

Dear Uncle Sam

He's not your type.
He kisses men with eyes
open, talks with them
shaded or averted
to acquiescent asses.
When cordoned
& questioned, he laughs.
Beware. His laughter beguiles.
Beware. He never shoots
straight. Always curls
fetal in the arms of any one
who can still him. Never sleeps
alone. Give him a gun,
& he may turn it into a prop
for a plié. Give him a gun,
& he may turn it on himself
& every fool who believes you.
He's claimed bodies in every
major city east of Chicago, saw mine
heaving among strobe-lit throng
& marked me: his sweat clinging
to my nape, our silhouettes
on bedroom walls,
now a mirage blurred
by desert dunes, now
only the caress of lines
hardened hands scrawl:
I'll be home next
month… I'll be home
next year… I'll be
 …I'll …

Tarry

Two oceans away from this bed where I seethe,
where just one touch from my holy trinity—

mother, sun, you—eludes me, an 18-year-old
Nepalese boy with ebony waves framing his fixed face

taps faithful callers on bowed heads & supplicant palms. He
neither moans nor mumbles a word, yet each spirits away

from his feet. *I just got a chance to see God!* one beams.
They say he is Buddha but to me he is just God. He looks

more like you to me: the one who heard *Please, don't go!*
in this bed, all night, before you left for a wilderness

I've never found. Maybe I'm reaching here for
the frazzled hem of your Army fatigues, to unravel

the ironies of too-perfect hair, your stoic gaze frozen
like a Daguerre we could have been, the twitching corners

of your eyes & perked ears betraying the focus on us & ours,
to muss out the how & why & what-if we never could.

The darkest hour's just before dawn, Mama would hum on
mornings like this when daylight saving time kept my beloved

sun at bay & I came crawling into Daddy's empty space
in their bed. I was a boy longing for schoolbooks

& Bible verses to spirit me away from myself then,
from endless nights when not even her loving gaze,

her thumb stroking my forehead, could silence the rage,
the longing no god could save me from. *How do you lie here*

alone all night? Don't you wish Daddy didn't have to work?
I'd ask, my head resting in her lap. Beaming down,

she never said a word. Right now, in Nepal, scholars assure
the throng it's not possible for this man-child to have reached

Siddhartha's peak, that three years of meditation without food,
without touch, does not prove he is reincarnation's gift. Yet they come

by the thousands, tarry for hours for their moment of enlightenment.
He does not look into their eyes, does not acknowledge their pleas.

Right now, you sit in some Humvee, waiting to be blown
into some horizon I can't save you from. From its summit,

the sun shadows me in my prison. Night soon will cover
them in theirs, cover you in yours. We kneel. We wait.

Woe Unto You, Sons

I.
Send out your sons, the men
of Sodom insisted. Inhospitality?
Or the sin of knowing *please*
would never do? What is the sin
in wanting—not the pulse
of a man—but the satisfaction
of making disciple of his nameless
back or mouth? Take & eat, they said
then in that alley, they say in locker rooms
& warehouses & dance halls now, darkened
to shroud shame. Marvel at what is left
when flesh becomes adornment: legions
of men focused not on the firmness
of their feet but the assurance in the grip
of *I got you, baby* from the latest cynosure
who's taken Daddy's place, the ones
who can't forget the legacy of flesh burning
flesh: a pat of a shoulder in the bathroom,
a belt cracking, cracking. *What's my name, boy?*
What's your name, boy, what's your name? what's...

II.
Stop! Drop! Shut 'em down, open up shop!
Cloaked in pitch, mid-stairway, I watch
the maddened writhing in the Palace
basement. DMX grunts over my head.
My niggaz is wit. You want it? Come get it.
Took it, then we split! You fuckin' right, we did it!
Hips & biceps wend & flail, shake
the faggot out on the dance floor
above, grind him to bits on knees & backs
on the filthy cement floor. I want
one back, one mouth, to melt into an O
& call my name, to claim mine as his.

I am not welcome there or here. I leave
with one whose real name I do not know.
I kneel before him, lick the salt from every inch
of his flesh. Then, open as he comes again
& again. The scars, leaching afresh, burst
as I fall, face first, into the pillow, each memory,
not feeling the scrim of safety rend, the skin
against skin. Never soon enough, time
topples onto itself, the sun exposes us,
a tangle of limbs, behind his bedroom's shades,
& the wounds crust over, steeling me
into what feels like a kind of safety.

Oblation

Nights like this I miss

the control over   the surrender of

a man's next

breath   thought

his

will   last word

wends   breaks

in my throat

every sinew

bruised   kissed

please st st st st

stop   go   don't

just   leave

tell me

what   anywhere

you want   just breathe

we are climbing   every round goes

higher

can these bones live

anywhere   curl inside

here

I won't let you go   don't

please   go

I don't

love you so   I do

you so love

please   so

let me   I won't let you

go until   do you

you love

me   you

I   won't

let   you

go

until you

bless me   curse me

The Morning After

willows welcome fog's
embrace: its shadow   a lone
silver glove   a shroud

A Prayer for the Phlebotomist

I watch you draw blood out of me, then think of Moses
with his staff at the Red Sea. When you tell me I should see

the specialist you see, I wonder how you steady
your hand, hold your own fingertips fast around the head

of the syringe as it pierces through flesh that trembles,
eager to part with its enemy. There was a time, if you'd asked,

I would have spread-eagled for you like my pores do now.
Do your eyes betray you sometimes like mine, fixed on

some faraway promised land I know I will not live
to see? Suddenly, I understand why I never liked

Charlton Heston in DeMille's flick. His hands knew
what to do. But his eyes didn't show he understood

that force holding those Technicolor holy waters
at bay, didn't well knowing why the newly free struggle

to believe safety awaits on the other shore. You look
through walls papered with ads for pills doled

from hands like that movie star's, hands who believe
only in the power they can formulate. O

help me focus on that place you see beyond
the murky deep, stare death full-on & smile.

To the Green Polka Dot Muumuu
My Mother Loved to See Her Mother Wear

May you have cooled her while she dashed about
a too-hot kitchen full of children & long-gone children's children

May you have hugged her close, dodging that
no-good too-sweet have-mercy-fine drunk of a man

waiting at the head of their table, who made her a home
with his hands, gave her these children &

took in those he did not give, the youngest,
prettiest, not his own blood but his, all his,

this stoic & stately girl you filled
with gutstillness, how you rocked her

when the grandchild you
never knew lay shivering, helpless

May you know when this baby girl escaped
her baby boy's gasping to do what she could,

she found you, your musty, stew-caked,
bloody self, waiting, across the years

May you cherish the exultations you heard
& felt when you did all the mothering her dust

in some lonely overgrown plot could not
when you resurrected her & we all rejoiced

Cystoscopy as Transfiguration

Maybe because the nurse emphasizes he's married, his cockney coiled
        around each syllable, like the clamp he places around my head
        after its Betadine & Lidocaine bath.

Maybe because of the lick of his lips as he sheaths my lap
        in protective plastic, my shaft at half-mast, the rest of me shifting,
        as if he's the first man who's touched me there.

Maybe because foreplay & torture blur.

What are you, mahn, half-Caucasian?

I confess my messy ancestry, that I have been shrinking of late,
        his sterilizing strokes inspiring little change—wanting (or not wanting)—
        to help me rise again.

I won't let go until you bless me, I want him to say, eyes fixed
        on what I want him to want outside these walls, his tongue wagging
        between teeth & lips.

I want to be the spaces there, no, the phlegm that threatens
        to choke him, that he fights back, prepping me for prodding
        by another brother's hands.

As if his pleasure in having the best of both worlds—
        my desire, his manhood intact—are not enough.

Then his boss enters, her accent thick as my tales
        of watermelon seeds spit during Saturday porch communions,
        of tea cakes & lemonade as bittersweet

As wagon rides to town that had to end
        when Mr. Mack's old mule had to get rid of her heavy load.
        Heavy load, heavy load, I got rid of my heavy load.

& I am not consumed, her skin as pink as the bottom of my feet,
        my brother, struck dumb by my glory, the afterglow
        of those mighty-good-times welling in my eyes.

Giving Up the Ghost

My left hand jerks like a catfish, hooked but
not yet dead, all nerves. Must be the fever talking.

I scoot to the edge of the triage table,
wince as another shock shoots through it.

I only feel it when I'm sick. I should be sick
more often. I brace for another jolt, then another.

Daddy resists the urge to grab my hand
like he did as doctors sutured my forehead shut

when I was in third grade & two teens caught me
spying while they made out under the gym bleachers.

I hit my head on metal girders running away & didn't
notice the heat blinding me was my own blood until I rushed

into the din of the game, into Mama's arms & she spirited
me into the ladies room. At the hospital, Daddy promised me

two scoops of ice cream from Piggly Wiggly if I didn't cry
while he squeezed my spasmic hand. On the ride home,

I savored the vanilla & strawberry milk until it left my limp
wrist a sticky mess. I think it enjoyed that sweet sting, too,

another blessed accident. Now, the nurse asks questions
nurses must ask, & I nod when she mentions the intruder.

Daddy bolts as though caught by his Holy Ghost, like the time
in church he felt himself about to lose himself & rushed

from the deacons' pews for the door, quaking & gutted
but not quite gone. He collapsed mid-stride in the doorway,

arms flailing out of my sight. I have always loved watching
men carry on, loved ushering in the Amen corner, MaMary's hands

& lap within reach there. I couldn't break his fall. I watched
his legs twitch, his brogans hanging onto his heels,

until he gave up his ghost, rider & ridden no more.
It's always been this way with us, watching from afar

as the other falls over himself, possessed by something
in some holy face calling us away from our right minds,

our bodies, our manhoods' limitations. When he bolts now,
I'm sure he's going to finally make a run for it & get away,

not look back, like so many of those I've loved
say their fathers did, like they ran from me before they knew

what they were missing. He flops back into his seat,
grabs its sides, then crosses his arms & collects his fingers

into fists. He slams his eyes shut in prayer, shivering,
as if crossing a street in a windstorm, intent on making it

to the other side. *O the blood of … O the blood of …
it will never lose …* By the time I fill out the consent form,

he has opened his eyes. He lets out a long sigh, smiles, then
laughs & places an open palm on my shoulder, then around it

to steady me as we walk to my hospital room. *It's OK, son.
Daddy's got you, & this ain't your time to leave here.*

Dust to Dust, Blacksburg, Virginia: Feb. 13, 2010

miss lucille,
it is the night before lovers
get free rein to love
and my neighbor is galloping
in his lover's lap
underneath my feet.
it is almost over. i hear
this pale rider gasp, reaching
for his next breath
in his lover's mouth.

i pull the zebra-print blanket
tighter around my shoulders.
this whisk of a town,
this home that never will be,
this room's cold concrete
have never warmed me.

now it is done
and i am swaddled in silence.
why and why and why
should i call a white man brother?
you whisper through the computer screen
and fill this room with your fire,
where carpet begs
for a long, hot bath
and sweaters and jeans yearn
to fold into one another,
arms and legs entwined.

if history prevails,
i, too, will die alone
and untidy, pulled apart
by the men whose call
for a ride i heeded,

who i handed my tongue,
arms, legs, and my last breath.
even then you will poet me home.
i am done with this dust. i am done.

Substantia Nigra

I pay a man to touch me now. In halogen he comes
to give what no other has. He bows at my bidding. He knows

where the burning leads, back to that thatched box, Florida,
one Saturday morn, not unlike the one that breached me

into song, to prayer without surcease, soundtracked by
that substantia nigra, that alluvial wealth whose terror deepens

with time welled in a phallic home of too many branches
of water & not enough swamps, home of broken

Spanish, moss, broken ballot boxes submerged
in swamps & locked in church halls, license to shoot

anything you fear or hate or fathom you own, if
you're light enough. It's the law of this No Man's Land,

licked dry by an unhinged ex-lover. Some call him Sun.
I call him enemy now. Now, I like it dark. I ran across

the border to clay, said here, take & eat, dammed God
for a bald, shiny head. Repent. Repeat. Said he'll do

till you come home. Said he hawks black art. I won't
be a hard sell. Just need a devotional ohm for my

objectification. He'll sit through my musings,
then surprise me with his intellect, punctuating

my sentences with his lisp. He'll savor my run-
on monologues. His genteel tongue will glide over

my fears. I'll swallow his sincerity. I'll pass it on.
He touched me & made me new that Saturday morn

I could not wait for you. I pay this soothsayer now
to quiet my Cerberus, anoint my fearsome heads with oil.

I moan to silence his snarls, hum him to sleep. Ah,
this gray-scale world. Intractable. Tartarus for perpetuity. O

Florida, O Panhandle, you penal colony, you haven
of anonymous alms & arms, welcomed in pitch, home

of the men who made me wish for the womb that made me
& the ones who made me wish I had one, had the heft

to bear the weight of this needling head, this water breaking,
this grazing with the ones who gaze East daily for the first,

the man who will never be the only one, whose pining primes
our quest. I pay my medicine man, that doubting Thomas,

that one with archangel name & face, to limn what keeps us alive
& welled but not spilling, not black or white or blue enough.

These wise men say I must tell you here, again & always,
I'm sick, I'm saved by their hands. Otherwise, other men

will lock me in a steel box. A man, a white one, did once.
T'was dark in there. I escaped doing what he forebade.

Screamed *I am a man, I am …* I refuse his bitter pills.   Still.
O Doctor Jesus, part this endless sea of doctors, of men's sin-

sick vision of these scars. O mirror of my mind, here, now &
forevermore, I am not pocked. These marks, not beast stings.

These broken bones are broken bones, do not portend or pretend.
Black men not mannish among black men know how to be solvent,

Sister, Sugar, Mama, Chula, Rahab, saint, wring the taint out, where
to tuck the bleach, how to cover blotches, slice edges, cinch waste

in translucent bags. I left mine on Mama & Daddy's front porch.
The dust mites won't touch it. The might-bes can't. Ah,

I've lied. I never left you, Marianna. I am that boy, that man
in this mirror, more than enough to touch what no man can. I am

that woe man, too. I ring an other. In halogen he comes. We sing
Negro spirituals. It's a black woe man thing. *I told Jesus, be all right*

if he changed my name. Too many deaths, too infinitesimal to many,
though I'll never stop counting. Tonight, I take this ringed man.

He leaves me wanting you wanting me. Who knows the way
to Canaan? Got my ticket in my hand. I ain't got time to die.

Ars Poetica: Nov. 7, 2008

...mutts like me
—Barack Obama

I am the what-are-you.
I am the brown, the red, the white, the sometimes blue.
I got some Indian in my blood.
I got some cracker, too.
Where I'm from, cracker is a badge
men wear like nigga in some 'hoods.
I am neither & both simultaneously.
My family owns the land
on which my family was Massa & slave.
The crackers don't claim us anymore.
The niggas never did, too uppity for their shelved lives.
I don't know what tribe I'm from, Indian or African.
My family never thought it important to note,
& I cannot afford Dr. Kittles' tests yet,
but when I can & his people read my blood,
I'm going back to Africa, just like the crackers
in my parts told me to, to see
if my people there recognize me.

The Mascogos here already reclaimed me,
though our people voted us away.
Although I've lost a lot of melanin
& some of my native tongues, I'm going to offer
my people the ones I've remembered. I'll tell them
Soy su negro hermano más oscuro.
Soy vasto. Contengo las multitudes.
They'll understand. I knew that language
before I knew I knew that language. It came naturally.
So did my crush on my high school teacher, Señor Herrera.
He called me his *hijo.* I never got the nerve
to call him Daddy, except in my dreams.
Señor Herrera had a nice ass. I am an ass man.
No worries. I have never been a nymphomaniac.
These days, HIV keeps me on an even keel.

I am often left alone with my thoughts in my one good hand,
with this charge to keep, this god to glorify.
I am mastering the power of positive thinking.
I have had three decades of practice. I learned the power
of the mind when I ignored my left arm, hanging limp
like a tattered flag in my pledge of allegiance
with tennis racket, trumpet, piano, pen,
computer keys, backs, faces, hands & feet.
I have kneaded them, cupped them, held them,
watched them walk away whole & leave me
bereft & free. The fingers I could move
reached what no one else could,
& everyone in my path marveled,
even my crackers & my niggas.
Then one night I met a lawyer,
another *inteligente* man with a nice ass,
who said *I can't get fucked by a cripple,*
& I've been trying to un-cripple my mind
ever since from wondering if Erb's palsy
is why Johnnie & Jason couldn't
love me outside our darkened bedrooms' walls.
I speak their names here, now,
because my finikin, airy god
doesn't speak in elliptical verse.

I need to tell you something. I am not
your paragon, your darling geisha boy.
I am not here to entertain you. I am not dying
with AIDS. Doctors call my mixed blood
a blessing, say I'm especially equipped
to fight this intruder, my comforter,
whose embrace may blind & maim me.

See. I am not afraid of facing you, or me,
or the notion of *we the people* anymore.
I am your darker brother.
I am vast. I contain multitudes.
I am the what-are-you.
I am the brown, the red, the white, the sometimes blue.
& I am all-American.
What are you?

Coda: Ars Poetica Nigra

Learn a strange language & its stranger
god. Praise him & other white saviors
early & often. Be broken. Stitch secrets
into your mask's lining. Grin & lie
to your children. They will demand
your freedom, & when you think
you have it, chronicle your journey
Uptown, down on U Street & all
over Bronzeville. Let Jessie B.,
little Annie & Miss Rosie show
you around. Try the Midwest on for size
through Grandma Beulah & her man's eyes.
If you are brave, venture South again. Rest
a little while in Bogalusa. Bask in its magic
& sin. Tell me: What does your mixed blood,
soaked in the Mississippi, peal? I need to hear
you blister, erupt & heal. Be reeeeeeeeeaaaal black
for me. Make nigger a dirty word. Use it as much
as possible. Kill the nigger in you.
It's a revolutionary act. Let me feel
what it's like when a woman loves
a woman: black as coal, black as love
is bittersweet as cane: how it feels to be a man
who puts a ring on another's manhood
before he gallops inside. Make love
they call nasty pretty, honey. Sing!
Write me loose. Make me dusky.
Scour our backyards, littered
& glorious. But beware the mutts
you find there. We can pack a mean bite.

NOTES & ACKNOWLEDGMENTS

NOTES

The book's epigraph is from Rilke's *Book of Hours: Love Poems to God*, translated by Anita Barrows and Joanna Macy.

Lyrics on section break pages are from "I Got the Love of Jesus," a traditional Negro spiritual; "Millions" by the Winans; and "The Blood Will Never Lose Its Power" by Andraé Crouch.

"Prelude: I Can't Help It" was written after the Michael Jackson hit from 1979's *Off the Wall* that inspired it. "The Morning After" was written the dawn after Jackson's death.

"What of a Body" juxtaposes a phrase common in many spirituals with a homophobic phrase made infamous by Buju Banton in his 1988 hit "Boom Bye Bye."

"It Could Happen to Anyone: A Letter to the Boy" was written after reading Jericho Brown's "Track 1: Lush Life" from his debut collection, *Please*.

"What Did You Do to Yourself?: Finding Fault" answers the question I am asked, more often than not, when people notice my left hand's paralysis due to a congenital brachial plexus injury. I live with the resulting condition, Erb's palsy.

"Resurrection Sunday": According to James R. McGovern's account of Claude Neal's murder in his 1982 book, *Anatomy of a Lynching*, on October 19, 1934, Neal, 23, an illiterate black man, was arrested for the murder of Lola Cannady, 20, a white fellow resident of Greenwood, Florida, who was his childhood playmate and presumed lover. Neal was coerced into marking his X on a letter of confession after his mother and aunt were arrested. He was taken to jails in nearby towns, reportedly to protect him. But, on October 26, a lynch mob that included Cannady's kindred (and allegedly members of Jackson County law enforcement) was allowed to take him from the Brewton, Alabama, jail back to Greenwood, where he was tortured for half a day, forced to eat his penis and testicles, and further mutilated to the point of death. What was left of Neal was dragged several dozen miles to the Jackson County Courthouse in Marianna, Florida. Along the way, his body was shot, stabbed and run over. Having read about what was to transpire in newspapers far and wide, including in *The New York Times*, several thousand men, women and children from across the country gathered for what was called a "picnic," whites' code name for "picking a nigger" to lynch. Fingers, toes and pictures of Neal's mutilated body were sold for sport. Neal's corpse was left for a spectacle until the morning after his death, a Saturday, when his body was cut down from a tree that remains in the town square today. Blacks were infuriated by what had occurred and fought back until Governor David Sholtz called in the National Guard to suppress what was deemed a "riot." No one was or has been arrested for Neal's lynching.

"Lost & Found in Tallahassee":
Eres uno de nostros: "You are one of us."
Eres un Mascogo: "You are black Seminole."
Soy un americano negro del Florida: "I am a black American from Florida."
Esto es nuestro hogar, también: "This is our home, too."
¿Qué se les gustaria decir a los estudiantes?: "What would you like to say to the students?"

"We Do Not Know Her Name" and "Drapetomania: Morning Dew": Chief Osceola's wife, Che-Cho-Ter (Seminole for "Morning Dew"), was captured and re-enslaved circa 1835. Legend records that she killed her captors, then herself, with hopes of preventing more skirmishes from erupting between Seminoles and slave catchers. Instead, her death and related events set off the Second Seminole War, the longest on U.S. soil. After it ended in 1842 and a third war ensued a decade later, thousands of natives from a number of nations, including more than 500 maroon blacks, were forced to flee their homes in the Southeast and seek refuge out West. In the late 1990s, as Seminoles and other members of the Five Nations were awarded hundreds of millions of dollars by the U.S. government, they voted to exclude blacks claiming Native ancestry. They have reaffirmed their votes consistently in the decades since. In 1851, Dr. Samuel Cartwright defined drapetomania as the supposed mental illness that befell blacks who fled slavery.

"You Da Only Man I Loves, Daddy: Lot's Daughters" contains an epigraph from "It Ain't Necessarily So," an oft-covered song first featured in Gershwin's *Porgy and Bess.* It is after Sterling Brown's "Slim Greer in Hell."

"Picky: Izola Ware Curry" was written after a conversation with poet and history buff Carlo T. Paul and uses excerpts from Curry's statements to New York police on Sept. 20, 1958, hours after the then-42-year-old, unemployed domestic stabbed Martin Luther King Jr. in his chest with a letter opener at Blumstein's department store in Harlem, where King was signing his new book, *Stride Toward Freedom: The Montgomery Story*. Doctors say if King had sneezed before the opener was removed, it would have punctured his aorta, almost assuredly killing him. Curry was diagnosed as schizophrenic and sent to Matteawan State Hospital for the Criminally Insane.

"HeLa" contains excerpts from a traditional Yoruba chant meaning "Mother, chief of woman's mysteries. Mother. Mother. Spirit. Spirit. Mother, give me abundance. Make it so. Make it so."

"An Atlanta Hustler Confesses…" is after Ai's "Killing Floor" and references Marvin Gaye's hit single "Sexual Healing" from his final album, 1982's *Midnight Love*. In October 2002, a 25-year-old black gay prostitute, Howard Belcher, went on a month-long spree, killing men he met at or around a Midtown Atlanta bar. He was sentenced to life in prison in June 2004. His victims were found bound with ties, beaten, strangled and asphyxiated with gas from their home's ovens. At one arraignment, he shocked the courtroom by requesting that he be executed. This poem, inspired by his story, also incorporates narratives of other sex workers.

"Touch" was written after Terrance Hayes' poem of the same name.

"Legion: Human Immunodeficiency Virus": The poem riffs on Aretha Franklin's "Ain't No Way" from her 1968 album, *Lady Soul*.

My beloved great-aunt sang "Blues in the Night," Johnny Mercer's oft-covered 1941 hit, and Muddy Waters' 1955 hit "Mannish Boy" with me and my grandmother almost daily in my childhood. "Ghazal of the Naptime Blues" and "Life After Death" feature refrains from these blues classics.

"A Patch of Blue in Tenleytown":
familia: family
Esa sonrisa ir, por favor!: "That smile to go, please!"
mi hermana: my sister

"In Search of Abe in Dupont Circle": *The Intimate World of Abraham Lincoln* is C.A. Tripp's oft-disparaged book alleging the 16th president of the United States had homosexual tendencies.

The title "Woe Unto You, Sons" is a remix of a refrain in Matthew 23. The lyrics in the club scene are from DMX's "Ruff Ryders Anthem," his hit from his 1998 major-label debut, *It's Dark, and Hell Is Hot.*

"Dreamboys" re-imagines moments from Tom Eyen's "It's All Over" from the 1981 musical *Dreamgirls* and Bob Merrill's "Don't Rain on My Parade" from the 1964 musical *Funny Girl.*

"Oblation" was written after Remica L. Bingham's "Topography" from her debut collection, *Conversion.*

"Cystoscopy as Transfiguration" was written after a one-sitting reading of Quan Barry's *Controvertibles* and features lyrics from "Heavy Load," a spiritual made popular by the Mighty Clouds of Joy.

"Substantia Nigra" re-envisions lyrics from the Negro spiritual "I Told Jesus," as performed by Roberta Flack on her 1969 debut album, *First Take.* The substantia nigra is the largest nucleus in the midbrain and is an important player in its function, in particular, in eye movement, motor planning, reward-seeking, learning, and addiction.

"Ars Poetica: Nov. 7, 2008" references Langston Hughes' "I, Too, Sing America" and Walt Whitman's "Song of Myself," both translated in Spanish, and Wallace Stevens's "Like Decorations in a Nigger Cemetery." Its epigraph is taken from President-elect Barack Obama's first press conference in which he was asked about his family's search for a hypoallergenic dog.

ACKNOWLEDGMENTS

Many thanks to the editors of the following publications, where earlier versions of poems appear or are forthcoming, noted here as they are titled in the original publications:

African American Review: "Family Reunion, 1993" and "To the Green Polka-Dot Muumuu My Mother Loved to See Her Mother Wear."

Black Gay Genius (anthology): "I Can't Help It" and "Ratiocination."

Callaloo: "Times Like These: Marianna, Florida" and "Picky: Izola Ware Curry."

Cave Canem Anthology XII: 2008–2009: "The Morning After" and "Ars Poetica Nigra."

Connotation Press Online (guest-edited by Honorée Fanonne Jeffers): "Finding Fault," "In Search of Abe in Dupont Circle" and "Giving Up the Ghost."

Crab Orchard Review: "We Do Not Know Her Name" and "Lost & Found in Tallahassee."

Cream City Review (selected by Quraysh Ali Lansana): "Ratiocination," "A Prayer for the Phlebotomist" and "Cystoscopy as Transfiguration."

jubilat: "I Can't Help It."

Los Angeles Review: "Legion: Human Immunodeficiency Virus."

Lambda Literary Online: "In the Lion's Den" and "What I Should Have Told the Homeless Man in Cleveland Who Mistook Me for Mary's Son."

Mighty Real (anthology): "What I Should Have Told the Homeless Man in Cleveland Who Mistook Me for Mary's Son."

Mythium: "Drapetomania: Morning Dew," "Chooseday!" and "Life After Death."

No Tell Motel: "*It Could Happen to Anyone*, or a Letter to the Boy," "Woe Unto You, Sons," "Tarry" and "Oblation."

Obsidian: "HeLa," "You Da Only Man I Loves, Daddy: Lot's Daughters," "I Am Black & Comely" and "Touch, or a Letter to the Mother."

100 Best African American Poems (edited by Nikki Giovanni): "Ars Poetica: Nov. 7, 2008."

Rattle: "Dreamboys."

Reverie: "Drive-by."

The New Sound: "Substantia Nigra."

TheThe Poetry Blog (guest-edited by Saeed Jones): "Dear Uncle Sam."

Tidal Basin Review: "June 26, 2009: The Morning After," and "Dust to Dust: Blacksburg, Virginia."

Vinyl: "Resurrection Sunday."

Thank you to Carolina Wren Press—Tanya Olson, who first read the book and said, "Yes, this one"; judge Lee Ann Brown, who has chosen it to herald; and president and publisher Andrea Selch, who has guided me to this rare opportunity.

In addition to selecting a poem for her anthology, I thank Nikki Giovanni for urging me to join her at Virginia Tech, which shifted the trajectory of my life. I carry your wisdom with me daily, and I am blessed to see how generous, how vast, your heart is.

To Remica L. Bingham and Jericho Brown, for taking my hand (and far-too-many bags) in New York and never letting go as we grow, thank you.

To Toi Derricotte, Cornelius Eady and Sarah Micklem, see what your vision has brought to pass! I am one in a growing body of believers in our individual and collective capacities to effect change in the world because we dare to speak our polyvalent, unapologetically black minds' subjectivities. Thank you for embracing me, for this wondrous gift, my Cave Canem family. Thank you to the staff past and present—Hafizah Geter, Marcus Jackson, Amanda Johnston, Alison

Meyers, Dante Micheaux, Carolyn Micklem, and Camille Rankine—for keeping us all connected and for your warmth.

To the editors and staffs of the Hurston/Wright and *Callaloo* workshops and especially to my first teachers, A. Van Jordan, Terrence Hayes and Tracy K. Smith, thank you for telling me those very bad poems had potential and for being present as I have tried to find the fearless voice you knew was hiding behind all the scaffolding I'd spent a lifetime erecting. To Vievee Francis and Gregory Pardlo, my most recent *Callaloo* mentors, you pushed me from master's thesis to manuscript, with laser-sharp insight, tenderness and hearts of investment and faith in the work. Thank you.

To my Cave Canem and Cave Canem South workshop and craft-talk leaders— Kwame Dawes, Thomas Sayers Ellis, Nikky Finney, Terrence Hayes, Angela Jackson, Colleen J. McElroy, Carl Phillips, Claudia Rankine, Ed Roberson, Ntozake Shange, Patricia Smith, Natasha Trethewey, and Frank X. Walker— I've learned with some of the best. What a gift! I keep your prompts, lecture notes, and advice close at all times.

Thanks, too, to my beloved classmates and friends in these aforementioned writing spaces and others, most recently at Virginia Tech and the Carolina African American Writers Collective, and to my friends in virtual groups who've cheered the lines you saw and especially interrogated the silences between each break. For fear of omitting anyone, I'll say to one and all, a deeply felt thank you.

To Randall Horton, for publishing my first poem and being a brother every step of the way, and to Katherine Sullivan, who's not only published my work but championed me being me at all times.

To Rachel Eliza Griffiths, you see and reflect the best in us! What a blessing you are!

To my professors and friends at VT: Virginia Fowler, who always has an open door to muse; Gena Chandler, who read and heard early drafts of many of these poems; Robin Allnutt, the best neighbor any poet-movie buff-bibliophile could have; Fred D'Aguiar, a tireless champion of "trying it"; Ed Falco, Jeff Mann and Lucinda Roy, who helped me cement a formal aesthetic foundation; Aileen Murphy and Paul Heilker, whose home and offices became spaces to literally

78

sing and cry my heart out; Erika Meitner, who asks the questions others dare not, always making poems stronger; and Bob Hicok, whose tennis matches were extensions of craft talks and class discussions about how to be "fierce" on the page. I owe Erika special thanks for sticking so close in the years since I left the mountains.

To mentors from the distant past at FAMU to this very present moment of doctoral study—Neel Ahuja, Genyne Boston, Mary Kemp Davis, Emma Dawson, Rebecka Rutledge Fisher, Joanne Gabbin, Tom Gardner, Minrose Gwin, Diane Hall, James Hawkins, Beulah Hemmingway, Mae G. Henderson, Vivian L. Hobbs, Karla F.C. Holloway, Valerie McEachin, Fred Moten, Margie Rauls, Joe and Louise Ritchie, Robert Ruggles, Ruth Salvaggio, Valerie White, and Roosevelt Wilson—you've been so right, and I am so grateful.

To the soul-kin who've helped me do the heartwork to get here whole, so much love: all of my church families, Daaiyah Ali, Leon Amos, DeShawn Artis, Tiffany Black, Khalilah Boone, Aaron Byrd, Carina Callier Brown and family, LaMarr Jurelle Bruce, Dawn Burkes and family, Elizabeth L. Butler, Sheila Carter-Jones, Adrienne Christian, Lea-Anné Crowder and family, Shalanda Coleman, Colena Corbett, Jessie Ray Cunningham, DéLana R.A. Dameron, James Dent, Rodreekus Downs, Paris Eley, Raina Fields, Katti Gray, E. Gale Greenlee, Wiljeana and Marshaun Glover, Efferen V. Hardnett, Reginald Harris, Sharon Harris and family, Diane Hawkins, Anaré V. Holmes, Jason Isaac, Lauren Jensen, Vincent M. Johnson, Amanda Johnston, Kenneth Jones, Robin Coste Lewis, Randall Kenan, Tara Lake, Judah-Micah Lamar, Aaron McKinney, Nicole and Deon Middleton, Darnell L. Moore, E.A. Moore, Bryan Murray, Eddie Ndopu, Maria J. Obanda, Nneka Otim, my Phantasique Five comrades (Darrel Alejandro Holnes, Saeed Jones, Rickey Laurentiis and Phillip B. Williams), Marcos Pope and family, Twyla Roulhac and family, James Ross, Charles Shackelford, Johnnie Shaffer, Stewart Shaw, Evie Shockley, Sarika Simpson and family, Cassander L. Smith, Ron Smith, Lolita Stewart-White, Regina T. Stone and family, Lisa Tabor, Anthony Treadvance, Robert Walker, L.A. Warren, Maya Washington, Marvin K. White, Camille Williams and family, and Betty and Roland Womack.

Most important, to my first family (Mama, Daddy, MaMary, Tudda, Twana, Cherise, Jerome, Derrick and all my babies), thank you for unconditional love and unshakeable faith; to my extended families—especially "the kids" who've become angels (Anthony, Blair, Cedric, Michael, Paris, Robert, Serapis, et al.)—I am because we were, if far too briefly; and to the One given so many names, I am because we forever will be.

The text of the book is typeset in 10-point Minion.
The book was designed by Lesley Landis Designs.